SAY, HAS THIS BUS BLOBBED, OR WHAT?

GRIT

A.H. STOCKWELL
PUBLISHERS SINCE 1898

Published in 2024 by
GRIT (Jill M. Holdsworth)
in association with
Arthur H Stockwell Ltd
ahstockwell.co.uk

A catalogue record for this book is available
from the British Library.

For Gordon Scade Silverwood and Mavis Silverwood,
and their wonderful words of enthusiasm.
In loving memory.

By the same author:

Natural Woman
Maybe Another Time When I'm Not Watching TV!
No one Invited Me & So I Threw My Own!
We Haven't Got All Night, Lass, So Keep It Short!

Contents

Contents (cont.)

Say, Has This Bus Blobbed, or What?

Written between 2009–2015

ALL TUMBLE DOWN

It's getting lighter and whiter.
Somewhere up there.
She's fighting all its power.
Stop the light, white!
It's driving her insane.
It's closing in on her.
It's hanging over her.
No air.
No space.
They flicker, fast and furious.
A sudden crumble of black and white.
She's left in the dark.
She reaches to feel your face.
Are you there?
Everyone is watching?!
Take her hand.
Lead her to a place where
she and her unborn child can rest,
a place where the fire in her eyes
once more will crackle.

NIGHT FEVER

Panic at the disco
When the lad you fancy moves in on another chick,
When the lights flicker,
When the beer runs out,
When Doug is marched out by a six-foot tall copper
for pushing ecstasy again,
When the DJ passes out,
When the girls' toilet is bunged up with toilet paper,
When you know you'll have to queue for hours for a taxi home!

CINDERELLA ROCK-A-FELLA

Cinderella rock-a-fella.
She had been to many balls already.
But, there were not going to be any more of those.
Just pots and the floor and a cruel world.
And, the gowns would end up being cropped or snipped.

She left in a rush when the clock struck.
She left no glass slipper, but the whole wardrobe.
Babes and papers and off down the road,
with petrol and a low profile.
Over and out.
Cinderella drop-a-fella!

DISPOSED TO TEMPERAMENTAL VARIABILITY (AS CHARGED)

A day like any other in the life of…
I got up.
I looked in the mirror and decided to make a change.
Hope is in my hands.
For every time he tries to break me down,
you got me, I got you," she says.

Stood up for my (their) right.
"And not a penny to her name," they say.
She put them on this earth, but he'll take 'em.
Them poor kids, they'll never have it proper!

They used to lock 'em up, you know.
Little women like this.
"Stark raving bonkers she is," they'd say.
In the good old days that is.
Falling drops upon falling drops.
A constant state of intense frustration.

As others before him he likes the act of instituting.
To hand over as for safekeeping.
From (once upon a time) straight-laced to
(once and for all) strait-jacketed, if he has his (wicked) way!

If the world just throws me off the edge…
Just remember who's still around, since
"I've just got three words to say to you: I LOVE YOU," she says!

WILD FRONTIER

The day is my enemy.
It can get nasty!
Bring on the night,
when below zero heroes can repair.
Licking wounds of hunger like games.

DEDICATED TO THE PRODIGY

HER PRIDE AND JOY
(PEACOCK 2)
(INSPIRED BY A PAINTING BY SIRI BJERKE)

Breathtaking beauty.
Up to her eyes in pomp and circumstance.
A pure fanfare.
A queen for any season.
A bride, in fact.
A feast for the eye,
not for the plate (this one).
Perfection in a less than chaotic world.
Radiance!
A spray in all directions.
A shower of bright white.
This peacock undoubtedly reigns.
Captivation of my feelings,
senses and everything that moves and hurts.

ANOTHER BRICK (IN) FROM THE (BERLIN) WALL
(1989)
(20 YEARS ON)

Humpty Dumpty sat on a wall.
That is until they pulled it down.
Not brick by brick,
but fast and furious(ly).
The balloons went up.
Mass euphoria!
Then Humpty Dumpty had a great fall.
Him and the rest of them who were sat on it.
Those with joy in their hearts.
Those with tears in their eyes.
Those with 'Sekt' in their bottles.
Those with hands that shake.
Those with praise (be to God) on their lips.
Then there was animosity!
They didn't just pop the cork,
they proceeded to burst the bubble.
All the chancellor's horses and
all the chancellor's men saw to it.
Let there be exploitation!
Some fell on their feet.
Some fell on their knees, most probably.
Some fell on their faces, and flat.
So Miss East was finally meeting Mrs West.
Here today, gone tomorrow was (not) just the job.
Tangible paybacks were the estates and what they were holding.
But they didn't get even ever again.
Couldn't put Humpty together again.
A total eclipse of the Communist heart.
Three in and seven out.
The place is whole alright and
united they do stand,
but divided they gain.

YOU COULDN'T WAIT

Sorry we didn't quite make it.
They say, it's understood.
They say you were a very fine man,
That you had a wonderful voice,
That you had a lovely smile,
That you had a great sense of humour,
That you had an infectious laugh,
That you were a great companion,
That you were dedicated,
That you had courage.
Every word is true.
But, there is much more.
You were a true gentleman,
An able sportsman,
A Yorkshire man.
You were loyal beyond reproach.
You had V.I.P. friends.
You were smart (in mind and appearance).
You saved lives.
You were unbelievably modest.
You worked all hours.
You did us proud.
And you were proud of us in our many different ways.

But, above all, your strength of will
was an inspiration.
We fought… the good fight, but we shared more.
I loved you very much, dad.
I feel such pain at my loss,
'cause trains and boats and planes can't take me there.
And nothing can console.
Watch over us, if you will.
You made your mark,
but your work is not yet over.
So, take care until we meet again
some sunny day.

IN LOVING MEMORY (DERRICK HOLDSWORTH 1932 – 2009)

ALL ABOARD!

All aboard the bus.
The special bus.
Not just anyone gets a seat.
His is reserved and has been for a while.
It's right at the front where he can see.
It's where he can see the finish line.
Where the race against time stops.

Ticktock.
The mouse beats a retreat.
No more clocking in or clocking out.
No more clocking up or clock watching.
No more clockwise or clockwork.
But entrance via the great Pearly Gates,
where not just the pearly kings and queens gather.

And if he sees my dad tell him, from me,
to give him a big hug!
He's the one in outfit of black trouser
and striped shirt with purple.
His favourite.
He'll find him chatting.
Just look for Pavarotti.
Another favourite (after Our Maker).
One of his biggest followers.

IN MEMORY

THE BURNING QUESTION
(2013)

They do roll around, don't they!
These days in the lives of women on a global scale.
Tell me again, when was the plan for us to be equal?
Best not to hold it!
Well, we've got the opportunities, have we?!
And there's fair play, is there?!
Did they/we actually forget about the fair pay?!
Back burner?
Did we burn all our boats?
We're forever burning the midnight oil,
so did we just burn out (after endlessly burning our fingers)?!

TOO DAMN LATE
(INSPIRED BY THE USUAL SHOW / TOO DAMN LATE
VIDEO BY ANNA MARTINE NILSEN)

It's the 'usual show' of hands.
What should have been 'A' became 'D'.
She didn't make the grade.
You can fall down the stairs.
You can fall up the stairs.
Or, you can just remain on them.
A broken nail, but when the pain
was so big she felt nothing at all.
A far cry from the silver screen,
between the apples and olives in (NYC's) Little Italy.
There's just the silver shutter she lets down
at the end of each very long day.
As sweet as it gets.
No 'grand slam happy time' ahead.
Left there in the dark.
It's a cold and hard curtain.
Such is (life) showbiz!

ME AND MY SHADOW

Behind every good man there's a good woman.
Thus goes the saying.
One might say, "An even better one!"
But behind every good woman there's no-one!
Only the wall she had her back up against.
What still lies ahead?
More corridors, extra hurdles,
the unconquerable maze, the tunnel… vision!
And the light at the end of it?
Electric, just like the bulb.
Governed by the switch.
It's either on or off (most of the time!)
Exactly who governs it?
The political wing.
The law.
Belief.
The press.
Statistics.
The quota.
The network.
The web.
Pride and prejudice…
Sticks and stones won't break good bones,
but they'll be picked,
and will certainly take a knocking!

SEXISM

Manful.
Self-made man.
Modern man.
Manning.
Manhood.
One's own man.
Man-made.
Mankind.
And… kind to woman?

CALCULATED

Be good, or be good at it.
You never know who's listening!
You never know who's looking!

DOMINO

Give a man a mask
and he'll tell you the truth.
Give a woman a mask
and you really **won't** recognise her!

DAMSELS NOT IN DISTRESS!

NIKITA for girls who ride

* cock-horses to Banbury Cross (past),
  with rings on their fingers and (bells) boards on their toes
  (present),
* winning races,
* out storms,
* and tie (by day and night),
* straight,
* the wind of change.

THE LITTLE LADY IN THE CRIMPLINE DRESS

Grandma be nimble, grandma be quick,
grandma jump over the candlestick.
Well, she was certainly fit enough to!
And she was definitely quicker than anyone named Jack.
A harsh youth and loss of child didn't kill her
(although it had been rumoured for a time),
but made her stronger.
Petite, agile, as broad (Yorkshire) as they come
and with a good portion of grit!
Yorkshire to the core and headstrong to the hilt.
A very independent little woman.
So smart in her hats, dresses and coats,
and taken for younger.
Afternoons in the Veteran's Hut on a regular basis
to play the forerunner of bridge.
High teas and trips to the fair with us two little ones.
Entertained by TV and my stories of foreign lands.
Maker of wholesome dinners.
A churchgoer.
Her Majesty's telegram a sure bet.
But, Humpty had a (great) fall, and so did she!
She came tumbling down.
They did put her back together.
There's a way where there's a will.
In the end there wasn't…
Sadly missed, but fondly remembered,
the proud lady who always turned the other cheek.

IN LOVING MEMORY (EDITH HOLDSWORTH)

DELIGHT

The world is your oyster.
So, am I to believe that your everything
is the edible marine bivalve mollusc
having a rough irregularly shaped shell
on that plate over there?!

ARTICULATION

Well, I might not be God's gift,
but I definitely have a gift of God.
I'll sing a song of sixpence,
or any other amount.
But I still haven't been given the chance
to do it for my supper!

MICHAEL JOSEPH JACKSON
(LOS ANGELES / USA 2009)

There was the feast of St Michael.
And then there was the King of Pop.
He was 50.
He was still young at heart.
He had been so well accepted
by people and by the world.
But beauty is in the eye of the beholder.
And some no longer thought he was,
neither inside nor out.
For he liked his cake and children.

There was the robin that rocked.
There was the opposite of sunshine.
There was the opposite of don't have to be there.
There was Ben.
The was the opposite of safe.
There was the song about the soil.
There was Diane, who wasn't clean.
There was the opposite of good.
There was the sweet stuff you put on bread.
There was In The - - - - - - .
There was the reverse of white and black.
There was the personification of excitement.
There was Billie Jean.
And the (beat) list goes on!

He was born to amuse, to inspire, to delight.
He certainly had the look.
He had composition.
He got in position.
He made us feel high and
he made us feel humble.
It wasn't 1999 that was an extremely good year,
it was 1958, and not just for the wine!

But the best was still to come.
We did see it, but not live.
A true master of his trade(s).
His timing was immaculate.
His precision admirable.
He was destined to experience
a boom after that performance.
So sensational, so electric, so breathtaking,
so moving, so amazing.
So sad, isn't it?!

He was only supposed to sleep for a while.
But this dose was deadly.
And he didn't make the transport.
He sang, "What about us?"
What about him, I say.
He sang, "Hold my hand."
Who did?
Did anyone?
Is this it?!
We can be here one day
and gone another night, he sang.
He has gone too soon,
but he will never leave our minds.

IN MEMORY

COMFORT ZONE
(BELFAST / NORTHERN IRELAND 2010)

Not exactly my idea of it.
Not my specially preferred zone,
this danger zone.
I was wondering how long it would take
for the mouse to once more
crawl out of the woodwork.
They'll force the price of petrol up
if they keep throwing them.
A car driver's nightmare.
Why aren't they singing?
Not even older than my own.
I knew a Belfast child once
back in my chemical days in Central Europe.
Whatever will her mother be thinking,
being a resident still of this uncomfortable belt.
This must be plan B.
It cannot possibly be plan A?!
More pre-occupied with his rise in popularity
than the cause of the madness when interviewed.
Is this New Wave stuff?
It's not music and it's not German.
And if it's not peace,
what is it a process of?
Why aren't they playing
football, volleyball, basketball,
handball or any other kind of ball?
But not golfball!
They should kick this other variation
on a theme of golf into touch!
An echo of Owen's rapid rifle, yet again.
Distressingly hard-hit that piece of metal targeted.
Enough to make you cry.
The over 80 officers probably did.
One of the greatest cities in the world
if not for wave upon wave of bitter-sweet.

STRIKERS
(THE 2010 SOUTH AFRICA WORLD CUP)

I could see the hatred in his eyes.
I have seen it so many times before.
Familiar rivals.
It was the unlucky dip.
It could have been lucky.
And they sang.
It was melodious.
And it was passionate.
And then it stopped.
But it was what they so needed!
They were down, unjustly.
And they sank further.
Not even the knights could help.
It was history repeating.
But they should have been writing history.
They did try.
A right anticlimax after a right royal send-up!
But it was good footy, contrary to popular opinion.
And then they contemplated a chuck-out.
Wrong to blame him, the last man standing.
I'm no football expert,
but I don't need to be to see the wood.
Wasn't it 'all for one and one for all' once?
Don't make him the odd player out.
Not organised, not hungry and no great work ethic?
No 4-2-3-1 system?
But they were so striking
in their white and red.

ODE TO HELEN

I have known you for so long,
but yet I feel I hardly know you!
In the end our trains taking so very different tracks.
But I know enough about the good,
the bad and the ugly which escorted you.
They say that the good die young,
but you were still in the springtime (of life).
We spent our childhood in the street.
A little stern, you and me both, they probably thought.
Just more mature.
But we had our share of laughs, toffee, peas and pies.

We took a last cup of wine together long ago,
but there was no supper.
Food for thought is what I recall.
And now your supportive final words to me
in that holy place still reverberating in my ear.
You were down to earth.
You were firm with your heirs, the rest (of us) and in voice.
And you still knew (your) the stuff
you were unable to strut in the end.

Sorry not to be with you in body on this day of obsequies.
But in my mind I am so very present,
with your loved ones, as with mine.
Your intellect (spirit) is now ascending to a higher place.
But you will still be there in physique, momentarily,
surrounded by the softest and the most beautiful
of luscious petals in tincture of yellow and white.
In all your richness, calmness and serenity
you will be the Lady of the (last) Moment.

IN LOVING MEMORY

ENTANGLED
(INSPIRED BY THE PAINTING 'KNOT' BY ANKI KING)

We're tied up in a knot,
you and me, me and you.
Whichever way, we are entwined by
life's many phases and challenges.
Our lives are at arm's length
but we are related by the past,
affixed by the present and
united by the hopes for (a) the future.
Enclosed within that circle of one,
one love,
one life,
and the frilly rosette of loose ends.

IS IT STILLBORN?

Some stumble, some fall, some dance,
some sing, some cry, some drink,
some eat, some shout, some argue
themselves into the next year.
How ever you (choose to) make it into 2010
make sure you
give a lot,
laugh a lot,
smile a lot,
thank a lot for
a new beginning,
a new chapter,
a new chance
to show what
you can do,
you can protect,
you can influence,
you can pass on,
you can drop,
you can finish,
you can correct/adjust
on this planet,
in this world (of ours),
in this society,
in this club!

THE FRESHEST TIME

New beauty manifests itself
before our tired eyes.
A springboard from the darkness
as we set ourselves in motion.
April showers wash away our pains.
Bird call, lambkin, chickens.
Greenery and a green light of a blessing.

OMG – THIS COULD TURN OUT TO BE A RIGHT ROCKY RIDE!

HAVING A WAIL OF A TIME!

How time flies when you are
Being pumped with blue à la radio-active
And NOT enjoying yourself!

A SHOCK (TO THE SYSTEM)

What leaves you feeling like a tree trunk
has just been bashed into your chest (sideways),
Your armpit is being besieged by an army
of thicker-than-most needles and
Your arm is forever on ice?

A premalignant lesion operation!

A CHILD'S WORD

She was my pride and joy.
The leader of the pack.
Round and round I went.
But I didn't want another.
She was dolled up, I thought.
She was more interesting, I thought.
It was love at first sight.
And now I even look like her —
My favourite dolly.

Her hair went thin with combing.
My hair might go thin with something else…

THE LIFE-OR-DEATH IMPORTANCE
OF THE APPROACH

So you got yourself a death sentence!
Well, there is a glimmer of hope in this bleak picture.
Many have declared war on this disease.
And a lot are alive and (kicking) healthy.
It's the pooling of info to help others to
see the future, which helps.
It's the precise characterising and customising.
Who cares if it's drugs developed between
the 1950s and 1970s if they work?!
It's the intense dosing.
Get blasted with as much as you can stand.
Be 100% compliant.
You can't do 'half a job'!
As a mum one will always get him/her to
the (treatment) appointment,
but now (also) get yourself there!
They do their best, and then it's up to you.
Give it your best shot, and then some!
It's mind on matter, and then it's mind over matter.
Keep focused on what you're going through, and then get over it.
Even though the molecular characterisation might be primitive,
it's a killer on the loose!
People need miracles.
Do it for yourself, for him, for her, for them.
Do it quite simply because "You're worth it!"

FIGHT FOR YOUR RIGHT TO PARTY

This is where I heal my hurts.
And the fact that I always dance my feet off
shows how many I've got (to heal)!
And that's because I'm forever led a dance.
More's the pity that I am now grounded.
And that's because they have cut
the ground from under my feet.
I'm still no bone-shaker.
I'm known to shake my booty
and I have often shaken a leg.
I hope to boogie-woogie in the house
and to that 'House' again real soon!
And God is my DJ,
because I worship that music.

SIMULTANEOUSLY

Now tell me, who **else** can
hang up washing in the cellar
and have a head of hair
in the bowl (of suds)
in the bathroom at the same time?

TIME FOR THE CHOP!

Three (3) operations and six (6) treatments later —
Wasn't there an easier way to tell me to get a haircut?

SENSATION

It was a 'fish out of water' feeling at the start.
Struggle and strife against the dominance
which denies freedom!
Then, there was the amazing effect
of the treatment on (my) performance.
Eventually, a stillness after the storm,
followed by an air of unpretentiousness.
Now it's a 'diamond in the rough' sensation.

CRYING TIME
(OR SHOULD I SAY A BLUBBERING MESS?)

I'm walking wounded,
but with my head held high.
The pain is quite fearsome,
but the days do go by.

Family, friends (and foe)
tell me to brave it and keep smiling.
Of course I do, regardless of the fact
that others keep piling-

Paperwork upon paperwork to deal with,
the bulk of which is of a nature called 'finance'.
And all of this and more is making it very difficult
for me to merely suffer in silence!

WELL AND TRULY S(T)IMULATED

Lights down.
Music.
And… Showtime!
Cold hands working on me.
'X' marks the spot.
Lights off.
Lights on.
Cold hands working on me.
'X' marks the spot.
Lights off.
Soon to be like the man in the Break.
But this is no Prison (map).
Lights on.
Cold hands working on me.
'X' marks the spot.
Lights off.
Lights back on.
Smile, you're on candid (digital) camera!
And, it hums away to itself… and me.
But I'm not sleeping.
And, then la pièce de résistance:
Coffee and a waffle,
by courtesy of those Fellows who are Odd.

TOTAL RELOAD!

I'm on my way.
I'm making it.
360 degrees.
And I don't mean snowboard!
From kill to cure (?) in less than a year.
I took the poison and the wine.
They took the (my) blood, sweat and tears.
And I'll make it show alright!

THE SCORE

Nine (9) out of twelve (12).
What could it be?
His marks in the English test?
Her saves in last week's handball match?
Their votes 'for' (the motion)?
Ladies who stick to their knitting?
Finished projects before the end of term?
Villages wiped out by the hurricane?
Rejections?
Girls unable to do the splits?
Cases solved by the end of the year?
Dogs who survived?
Babies with blue eyes?
Shattered baubles after the Xmas tree came crashing down?
My fight to keep my health (and plenty more)?
Or, in other words, a test of my body and
soul (and a whole lot more)
over the past nine (9) months,
which I could have done without (quite frankly)?!

YOUR CHRISTMAS WISH NO. 1 / 2010

My first book.
It was supposed to be a 'collector's item'.
It is.
But so far it's only me and the publisher
collecting it!

YOUR CHRISTMAS WISH NO. 2 / 2010

My second book.
Ditto!

YOUR CHRISTMAS WISH NO. 3 / 2010

My third book,
which is lying over there (quite literally)
naked (without its cover)!

YOUR CHRISTMAS WISH NO. 4 / 2010

My pièce de résistance
which is bursting at the (its) seams
(full to overflowing with trivia
to be charred by critics),
to take the market by storm?!

YOUR CHRISTMAS WISH NO. 5 / 2010

My unfinished work.
Keep wishing!
Have a good one…!

IT'S GETTING HARDER EVERY YEAR!

"All I want for Christmas
is my two front teeth," he said.
All I want for Christmas
is my hair (back!)

ON DEATH ROW

A last request?
5 minutes to reflect on la (dolce) vita?!
5 minutes to cry for what was and just might have been?!
5 minutes to scream the place down?!
5 minutes to call and hug one's loved ones?!
5 minutes to wear one's favourite outfit?!
5 minutes to give that last piece of advice?!
5 minutes to laugh at all those jokes?!
5 minutes to listen to those favourite tracks?!
5 minutes to finish writing that book?!
5 minutes to pay that bill?!
5 minutes to delete those emails?!
All that in 5 minutes??!!
To have more than 5 minutes?!
I have!
And for that I thank my lucky stars...

LADYLOVE

To save a 'good' woman must be like
having the world in the palm of your hand.

TIME OUT

Will I be pushing up daisies?
Will I be pushing up dandelions?
No, I'll be doing push-ups
for as long as I can push the boat out!

CORRIDOR (OF UNCERTAINTY)
(INSPIRED BY THE VIDEO 'CORRIDOR OF UNCERTAINTY' BY IDA JULSEN)

Just when she thought she'd made it and was glad!
Just when she'd gone that mile,
there was an extra one.
It was disarming.
It was disconcerting.
Just get through that window.
Just remember that the grass
shall be greener on the other side.
Just for then burdened by a load, and life.
It was no beach, but those waves were surfed.
If she hadn't been up to her neck in it,
she might have resembled a fish out of (its) water.
But, never before had she felt something so XXL,
in the (scheme) misery of things.
Soul Force.
The arrogant edge of sheer focus.
It was like clarity to the condemned.
So sweet.
Like a blustery breeze.
A battery recharge?
A calmness in a sea of emotions.
Still 'alive and kicking'
but not the same…

WHOOPEE!

Blonde girls have more fun?!
What, you don't say!
Some girls don't know how
to have fun whatever the hair colour!

p.s. It takes a bit more than that…

EXTREME UPGRADE?!

"Enjoy the new you!"
Well, if I could get rid
of the uncompromising pain
that's riddling my body
and contain the sparks
I might be able to!
Don't hold your breath…

SMALL MIRACLE

Getting to Lillehammer hospital by bus before 9 am
after making ready kids for school and
in the state she is in right now
is like telling that man to take up his bed and walk!
He managed it, with a little help from his friend,
I guess she will too!

FIGHT YOUR OWN BATTLE

He had 10,000 men.
Here there's only speak of one.
When I'm up, I'm up.
When I'm down, I'm really down.
Lying down!
And there's no halfway up.
No neither up nor down.
It's all or nothing.
Total impact or ground zero.
Meaning, I'm in the land of nod.
I'm having tons of beauty sleep.
I'm having **40,000** winks.
A massive dose of shuteye.
I'm a sleeping partner, without the business,
'cause I'm not playing a very active role (right now).
Will someone tell me when this struggle and strife is over?!
When this battle is won?!

SELF-HELP

An apple a day
Keeps the doctor away,
And so does a smile
At yourself in the speil!

Speil = mirror

JILL'S TIPS FOR SURVIVAL!
(2014)

* Exercise/walk/keep active both during and after completing the treatments.
* Get fresh and cool (even cold) air/water, if possible.
* Don't completely stop doing things you enjoy (swimming, dancing, singing or whatever!).
* Eat well/healthily, if you can eat, to keep your strength up (and you need it!).
* Smile!
  Smile as much as you can, even if it is hard.
  It helps the whole body.
* Keep a sense of humour!
  It is so important to keep a sense of humour and to be able to have a 'chuckle'.
* Be strong (in mind and body) and 'take the bull by the horns'!
* Don't let your emotions get the better of you, but it is OK to cry sometimes.
* Motivate yourself.
* Play an active role and do it 'your' way.
* Make sure that you stick to the treatment(s).
  You can't do half a job!
* It's a fight (for the body)!
  You have to tell yourself to fight/to give it your 'best shot'!
* Make the best out of a bad job, be it the way you look, or... whatever! Be creative.
* Buy yourself something nice sometimes
  (small or big/big or small).
  It might/will cheer you up, and remember – "you're worth it".
* Get an attitude (the right attitude)!
  Tell yourself that there is always someone (somewhere) worse off than you!
* Live every day as if it is (not your last but) a gift!

If I can do it, so can you!
Good luck!

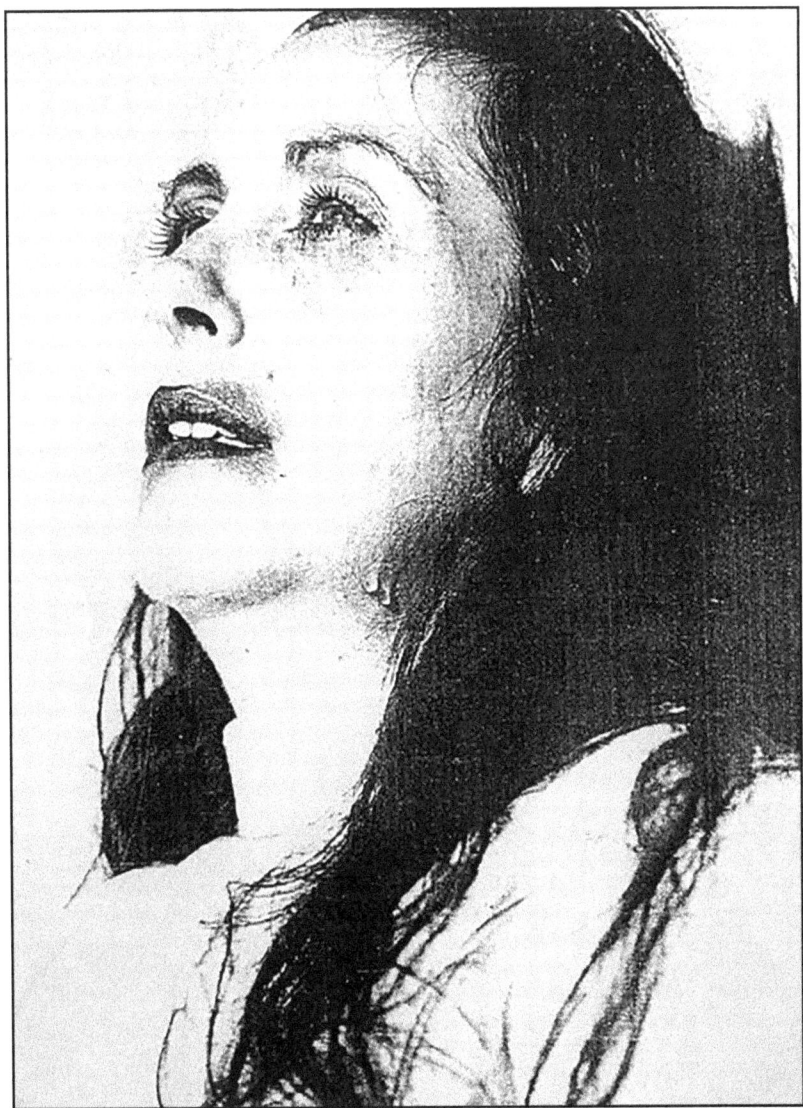

STILL ALIVE AND KICKING, AND SO RELIEVED...

A STITCH IN TIME
(MEN'S HEALTH)

A stitch in time saves nine.
Nine seconds of 'what if…?'
Nine minutes of hot and cold (sweats).
Nine hours of utter anxiety.
Nine days of questions and regrets.
Nine weeks of waiting to get something done.
Nine months of backbreaking treatment.
Nine years of getting over it.
The test might save you!
So, what you could do today shouldn't be put off until tomorrow.
Take the time off that nine-to-nine job.
Postpone the (football) training.
Drop the date.
Get off that sofa.
Get over the embarrassment.
Get stitched (up) with whatever it takes.
Avoid the 999 call.
Who knows, you may be able to continue
to be 'dressed up to the nines' (if you so wish)
for more than the next nine…?!

RIGMAROLE

Such is life – a stage.
Sometimes one treads well, sometimes one doesn't.
And even more incalculable,
one never knows when the final curtain
will actually hit the boards!

ON MY SOAPBOX

I don't wash my hair too often,
because I don't want water on the brain!
I can't do with a head full of suds.
I need a clear one, since my life
is already one big soap opera!

TRANSFIXION

Sometimes I think that
I'm the only one on this track.
It's rough and I'm constantly
pursued for my track record.
Of course, I have been off it and
I have been beaten, but
I will stop them in their tracks…

NEVER WALK ALONE

I've got my guardian angels up there
to see me through thick 'n' thin.
And my dad's leading the herd.

STAMPING GROUND

HOME is…

Where the heart is,
Where you can think straight,
Where you can spread out,
Where you still do not forget to use your manners (!),
Where you can breathe,
Where you can be someone else (if you want to),
Where you can cry,
Where you can dance your socks off,
Where you can recharge,
Where you can collapse (in a heap or otherwise),
Where you can hang up your mask,
Where you can wear your heart on your sleeve,
Where you can unfold your wings (creatively),
Where you can forget,
Where you can exercise your (inner) voice,
Where you can pamper your soul (mate),
Where you can show off (a little),
Where you can…
Be (always and forever) free!

IN THE FLOWER OF HER (YOUTH) POWER!
(BURMA 2010 / 2011)

Home is where the heart is and
it's usually home sweet home.
But she found little or no comfort in her own.
Her home was her castle
until her head rolled, like others before her.
Like Anne B.
B for beheaded?
B for bagged?
And there was this Mr American Dream.
Carried in with the tide, he was.
No room at the inn, but at hers.
Quite captivated by the captive,
with a love for blossoms, I'm sure.
There was no tide over,
but he did leave his tidemark.
A set-back after a secret set-up?
And they cried when they didn't let them see her.
Like Martin before her, she too
has a cherished hope.
It's called justice.
Or is it just ice?
All wind and water.
Like some big project without support.
But hers is with!
Well, it's certainly on ice.
For how long?
For quite some time, seeing as how
she has now been penned,
the little lady with the handbag!

ON THE HOUSE

Nothing is free in life, but
A smile when I see you walking towards me,
A hug when I know you need to know you're loved,
A kiss when I tuck you in and say goodnight,
A pat on the back when you act all grown-up and make me proud,
A wink when you need to know you should
take it with a pinch of salt,
A word of encouragement when you are wondering how,
A song of praise when you make the grade,
A blind eye turned (on occasion) when you make a mistake,
A yawn when you need to know that I am bored too,
A burst of laughter when you do 'your thing',
A frown when you wander off the beaten track,
A few kind words when you're apologetic,
A look of love when I see what a beauty you are turning into,
A pick (me) you up when you are treated badly,
A piggyback ride when you are exhausted,
A karate chop when we're fooling around, having a bit of fun,
A teardrop (in the ocean) when you need
to know how much I missed you,
The best things!

HOME IS WHERE YOU CAN THINK STRAIGHT!

Welcome be to those who enter with an open mind.
Welcome be to those who leave with an open mind.
Welcome be to those who don't try and enforce
the contents of their mind on hers whilst
engaging, enjoying, appreciating (?) the company of it!

TRAVELLER
(INSPIRED BY THE PAINTING 'TRAVELLER' BY ANKI KING)

Any which way but…?
Am I on my way?
Am I just dreaming?
Am I really
a bird of passage, a globetrotter, a gypsy,
a nomad, a rover, a trekker,
a voyager, a walker, a wanderer?
Will I hurt myself?
Will I hurt others?
Will I be confronted or even comforted?
Will I be alone or have sporadic company?
Will I find my feet or fall on them?
Will I neglect them?
Will I see the wood for the trees?
Will I feel the greener grass on the other side?
Will I get the best of the things in life which are free?
Will I be able to live and let live?
Will I believe in beauty and the eye of the beholder?
Will I (only) live but once?
Will I have regrets?
Is this the right thing to do?

NEIGHBOURLY
(NORWAY 2011)

The young man who fixed my buffets
is now 23rd in the world
when it comes to racing downhill
over a winding course
marked by artificial obstacles.
At least for now!
And tomorrow?

TOM
(2011)

The last man (standing) sitting
in Bischofshofen.
And, he won it!
He's no 'Sitting Bull',
although his approach is… bullish!
He's the first in the last 20 (x 12) from this soil.
And the conditions were
not as superb as his performance
by a long shot!

1500 METRES
(2011)

They fought like lions.
But someone had to lose.
He said he'd just keep going,
even if it hurt, our Mr B.
He did, and it must have.
Inside lane.
Outside lane.
Lap after lap.
Round and round he went.
So focused.
So much strength
in those thighs and ankles.

REGULAR OR JUST PLAIN GOOFY?!
(NORWAY 2011)

All the colours of jacket under the sun.
No sun on this day though, only on TV.
Stressed, impatient, laughing and straight faces.
In two lines.
There are big ones, little ones and mothers (holding it all up).
It's almost dark and the spots are on.
The clock's ticking and the queue's endless.
The man on the Bear Cat has a walkie-talkie
and his foot on the gas.
There are steaming noodles, chocolate, crisps and pop.
And there's rubbish.
But, then again, there's music!
Names in abundance.
Kids on snowboard.
Kids on two skis.
Kids on one ski.
Kids on no skis (just boots)!
Kids with sticks.
Kids without sticks.
Kids going backwards.
Kids jumping.
Kids curving.
Kids crouching.
Kids grabbing.
Kids driving straight down.
There's a front flip.
There's a back flip.
There's 180, 360, 540, 720 and…
It's getting hotter and there's the adrenaline rush…!
And then the fun stopped.
It was all over at 6.

SUNDAY (EVENING) ON MY MIND
(NORWAY 2011)

"I can feel it coming in the air tonight".
More snow!
Don't know where to put it all.
But it's beautiful, this thick, soft fabric of white,
which is packing itself into every nook and cranny.
Millions of diamonds sparkling and the cosy homes.
But down by the boats it's a different world.
It's like an 'underwater world'.
It's like something from Star Wars.
It's like a meeting ground for lost souls.
It's raw.
It's barren.
Total exposure to the elements.
The flashing light in all its greenness.
It's like they forgot to turn the one familiar thing off!
Bring on the dancing girls (on ice)?
Or is it, bring on the Martians?
Woe is he who left something open.
He won't get it closed now!
Woe is he who left something uncovered.
He won't get it covered now!
Roll on Spring and 'here comes the sun'!

LIKE LAMBS TO THE SLAUGHTER!

Poor Mary.
She loved being with those kids, albeit for a pittance.
And she would have made a good job of it
if only she'd had the training!
But, enjoy it whilst you can 'cause when you're trained…
you won't get it!
Sad state (of that community).

HERALDRY
(INSPIRED BY THE PAINTING 'ARMS' BY ANKI KING)

She was armed.
Prepared for conflict or any other difficulty.
Her reputation preceded her.
Imperilment with brief encounters, flashbacks,
flash floods, flashlights, flash points and news flashes.
A flash in the pan!

No elephant tears,
but tusks on the burning concrete.
Severance pay!
Remnants of imperialism rather than industrialism.

POMP AND CIRCUMSTANCE IN 2011
(THE MONARCH IS BACK!)

Britain's royal weddings are electric.
And we're good at them!
You can't make a mistake,
the world is watching, she said.
According to David C, it will be
a big day for the whole country.
The 'working' people take part in it.
They have a good time.
They open up their hearts to them.
That way since 1923.
And, even if it chucks it down
they don't care!
The adrenalin will keep them warm.
We're a reserved lot, but when we go for it…!
It's going to be a big deal.
Safe and sound for no less than twenty million pounds.

Traffic chaos since the early hours.
And we do know how to queue.
Waiting in line since 8.15 a.m.,
at the North Door of the home of
the Coronation since 1066, apart from two.
A place for the people.
They are all there, Westwood, Conran, Burberry,
McQueen, Parry, Rutter, Chaucer
and Mealor, in some shape or constellation.
And then there is David B, Victoria, Elton and Mr Bean.
The avenue of trees.
The hats.
The colour.
Something old, something new,
something borrowed and something blue.
And the best-kept secret!
Everything well and truly under wraps.
So, the princess for a day is to become
a princess for a lot longer.
Miss 'it should have been me' in the crowd
will have to hold her peace, or marry Harry?!

A sea of bobbing heads and flags.
Red, white and blue as far as the eye can manage.
British pageantry at its very, very best.
A surge of applause and cheer.
A storm of confetti.
Love is in the air!
A double take of 'seal it with a kiss'
by the Duke and Duchess of Cambridge.
A salute to one of their own,
which fell on her little deaf ears,
since she had them covered up!
A good day was had by all and all over.
A communal, unifying celebration
amidst a difficult world.
We were all glad!

THE BIGGEST OUTSIDE BROADCAST OF RECENT TIMES, LADIES AND GENTS! (2011)

Up to two billion viewers worldwide.
Well over 21,000 goodwill messages.
No less than 12,000 pieces of 'royal' china
collected by the lady in Australia.
An amazing 10,000 foreign broadcasters on site.
A total of 2,000 extremely distinguished guests at Westminster.
And they all rolled over and 1,350 fell out,
leaving 650 in the state dining room at the Palace.
And then they all rolled over and 350 fell out,
leaving 300 at the knees-up, which wrapped it all up!
And they all rolled over again and 298 fell out.
And then there were two, on a tandem
from Boris and the pride of London.
It will be a bumpy ride…
They will be in the limelight, spotlight
and just about any other light!
Still, if she's been in the Girl Guides she'll 'be prepared'!

WEDDING LUNCH 2011

MENU
FOR THOSE NOT INVITED BUT SCREEN-WATCHING
(AND ON A BUDGET)!

MAIN COURSE
Filet of salmon with drizzle of pesto and flake of parmesan
Smashed beans with mustard
Wedge of pitta

DESERT
Crêpe à la blueberry
Crème fraîche blob

DRINK
Orange fizz

STANDING TOGETHER
(NORWAY 2011)

(INSPIRED BY THE PAINTING 'STANDING TOGETHER' BY ANKI KING)

Standing together
in the springtime of their lives,
in the social conditions of classlessness and equality,
in their elected representation,
in the manifesto and words of wisdom,
in hopes for the future
and in laughter.

Standing together
in awe,
in the heat of the moment,
in fear,
in panic,
in the brutal reality,
in the force of (its) nature,
in the darkness and the cold.

Standing together
in shock,
in horror and talking without speaking,
in tears of grief,
in gems of roses and torches of brightness,
in minutes of silence and remembrance,
in national unity,
in the conviction that the vision
planted in their brains still remains.

Standing together
like a bridge over troubled water.

Standing together
in the forces of good which are all around us yet.

Standing together.

DEDICATED TO THE PEOPLE OF NORWAY

9/11 TEN YEARS ON (NYC / USA 2011)

It's not TGIF. Not, Thank God It's Friday.
It's TYO, Ten Years On.
And there is a great need for TLC.
Tender Loving Care.
Because the pain is still there.
It's still raw.
GROUND ZERO.
It's where so many of the 2,983 people
lost their lives.
Ninety countries lost somebody in the zoo!
Some died fighting (to save) and thus placed
so costly a sacrifice on the altar of freedom.
Some perished crying.
Some perished on the phone.
Some perished on the stairs.
Some perished jumping.
Some 'just' perished
when those great towers were brought to their knees.
A never-ending list of horror and sadness!
It changed him.
It changed NYC.
It changed America.
It changed the world.
The 9/11 generation of warriors.
Can't stop the memories flooding back!
I bought flowers there once.
I bought cookies there once.
I visited customers there once.
I viewed Manhattan from up there once (or twice).
I viewed **those twins** (in amazement) every evening
from that hotel window over the road and Century 21.
But what was I doing on 9/11?
What was he doing on 9/11?
What were they doing on 9/11?
What was she doing for the past 10 years (of aftermath)?
Not sleeping!
And Paul sang about the incredible 'sound of silence'.
I heard the pin dropping…
And then the Fire Department's 2,000 Harley Davidsons.
For the 343 firefighters who could have still been here today (of all days).
Let's roll, they said (as he had done).
And the torn Stars and Stripes, which had been flying then,
is proof that God Bless(es) America.

DEDICATED TO THE AMERICAN PEOPLE.

THE CONCEPT (OR BIG BANG)

As people
Move more freely,
Meet more freely,
Mate more freely,
The world becomes a freer place.

Free for
A free-for-all,
A free-hand,
Freehold,
A free kick,
Freestyle,
Free trade,
Freewheeling,
And none of this is quite as positive as at first glance.
Still, you can't put an old head on young shoulders!

It's free
To act at will,
Not to be under compulsion or restraint,
Not to be confined,
To be autonomous or independent,
To not be subject to conventional constraints,
To be other than exact or literal (in translation…),
To be unencumbered,
For some…
For him?
For her?
For them?
And therein lies the baffling crux of the dilemma!

p.s. In the case of lack of funds to 'free up', try for FLA
(Free Legal Advice)!

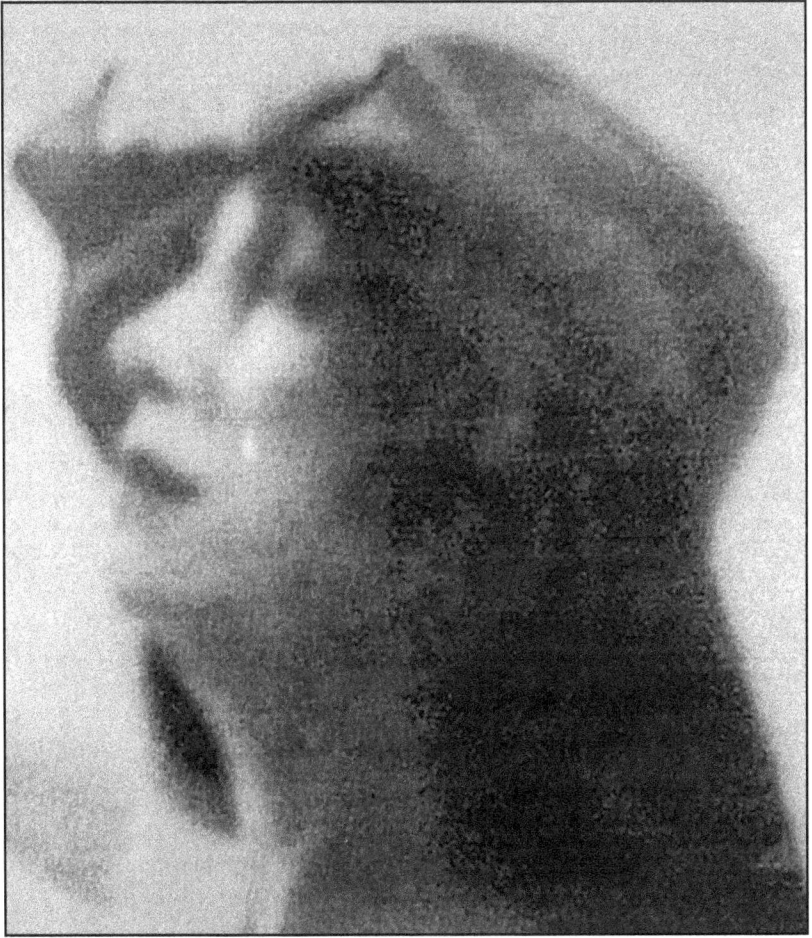

COULD HAPPEN TO ANY OF US!

FOOD GLORIOUS FOOD
(NYC / USA – 2011 OR ANYTIME!)

He wanted more.
Back in those days,
he was punished for it.
She doesn't get (hardly) any.
Now, in these days,
she is punished for it.
This way, that way and every other way.
A never-ending circle of doom and gloom.
Sidestepped, derailed, displaced…
No longer fast lane, but fast downhill!
What's the verdict against the former boss of the IMF to her?
What's the name of the richest man in the country to her?
What's the worst fall to date of the NYSE to her?
What's shop 'til you drop to her?
What's even 9/11 ten years on to her?
Nothing compared to her **glorious** days.
Do we ever stop to think?!
Her loss after loss in the land of the free, the land of the brave.
Well, she's free from any kind of…?
Obligation!
And she certainly braves it.
The American dream?!
Does she even have dreams?
One guess that she's NOT dreaming
of a white Christmas past, present or future!
It's like the cow jumping over the moon!
It's like Wee Willie Winkie running through
the town in his night-gown!
On that subject, where are her children
and her children's children?!
High on life!
Live your life!
Wear your passion!
And what was that again?
Very skinny, skinny and loose jeans.
She's lucky if she has (can keep) a pair,
the little lady huddled up at the entrance
to one of the busiest subway stations in the world,
and where the MAN has a HA(T)T on (A)N.

HIS SMILE LIT UP THE COLD WAR!
(RUSSIA 2011)

Sooner or later it had to happen!
From behind the Iron Curtain he journeyed into Outer Space.
The first man.
A journey (with Sputnik) to distinguish
the champs from the chimps, one might say.
He probably felt like a chimp,
but he was one hell of a champ!
Close to something unreal.
A prisoner and ruler.
It was so 'off the wall', fifty years ago.
The scream of reason?!?!
He could have been trapped in the ultimate ocean.
Swaying from side to side, going round and round.
Surrounded by nothing.
With only his smile to keep the stress at bay!

Everyone was watching on April 12th.
Impromptu, when things went wrong.
Believing in himself to the tune of 'nothing is impossible'.
He was about to traverse new territory.
So was I.
He was heroic, and it was historic.
So was I, and it was, in the mind's eye of my mum and dad.
Flesh is weak, and we ask for too much,
but it's a comfort when we get it (success),
and without paying?!
But how much did he actually pay (in sweat and tears)
for the highest honour?
Forgiven, but not forgotten, for departing
once more from this world and never to return,
Mr Yuri Gagarin.

IN MEMORY

SHEER DISASTER OR THIRD TIME UNLUCKY!
(JAPAN 2011)

A glimpse of hope?
A tiny little girl.
Alive and kicking.
Lucky to be reunited with them.
And they're working around the clock.
Too late for 10,000 and rising.
Devastatingly slow for millions.
The worst since World War II.
The hospital made it, but that's about it!
And he's trying to ride his bike through the rubble.
He's looking for the 15,000 minus 12,000 (in his town)
like some castaway on the moon.
And the neighbour's causing a stir.
We just don't need radiation treatment, they eventually sob.
On the scale of things, they gave Chernobyl a seven.
Is this really only a five?
They're very worried in Japan.
They're very worried in Germany.
They're very worried in Italy.
It's only the start of the panic wave…
Gas-mask mania sparks memories of
past war warriors and war waging
and war effort and war prisoners
and conscientious objectors.
And some are meeting to have coffee, waffles and a chat!
Not even the Sumo wrestlers could contend this.
Nature was deaf to reason, blind to consequence.
The Nikkei, a dirty Wellington boot splatter,
or some sudden manifestation change of a lie detector's needle!
No dial tone to start with.
No Facebook, no Twitter, nor anything else
which gets nervously excited.
And so now's the time to save power.
Turn them off, those enormous flashing screens and the trains.
There's no pushing or shoving for food and other things,
just helping and sharing.
And it's still rumbling, trembling, shaking.
Dust to dust, and yet more dust to dust.
No wonder those foreign students called theirs off!

DEDICATED TO THE PEOPLE OF JAPAN.

LOST PROPERTY
(JAPAN 2011)

She's got a brand-new pair of roller (skates) blades.
He got a brand-new (key) jacket.
She got a brand-new suitcase.
He got a brand-new PC.
They got a brand-new apartment.
Still, it's mind over matter now...
They're lost, but not found!
And finders will be keepers,
seeing as how the population has now been transformed
into little islands
surrounded in mud
on a massive scale.

MUSIC FOR THE NEXT (JILTED) GENERATION (2011)

All the world's a stage, still.
All the banking system's on fire or on ice.
All the globe's warming.
All the rubbish's reproducing.
All the Earth's cracking (up).
All the nature's losing its mother.
All the oil's running out (and not merely into the sea).
All the wind and water's clearing us out (and off).
All the race is losing the human.
All the data processing's filling our time.
All the telephone's controlling us, and I must think of Orwell.
All the House (of Worship)'s losing its pull.
All the custom and heirloom can's getting dated!
All the fitness wave's taking over.
All the television's becoming reality.
Is this all we can hope to leave them?
Or is there still sanctuary?
Or is there just money?
Or is there even money?!

DEDICATED TO THE PRODIGY

STAIRWAY TO HEAVEN

One year older,
None the wiser,
But one step nearer to God,
The maker,
The shaker,
The waker,
The taker,
Who Himself gave so much.

ASSISTENZA!

Take him to church.
Take him to bed.
Take him to the bathroom.
Take him to eat.
Take him to hospital.
Take him to the centre.
Take him to physio.
Take him to the park.
Take him to the bus.
Take him to town.
Take him to register.
Take him to apply.
Take him to complain.
Take him to court.
Take him to the cinema.
Take him to the dance.
Take him to buy flowers.
Take him to Tom, Dick or Harry's!

DEDICATED TO THE CARERS.

HUMANITARIAN AID

It seems to me like there's a whole lot more people who need it.
And I don't mean food and clothing!
What with an eye for an eye and a tooth for a tooth…
I guess that's why some people
have theirs in a glass (at night)?!
It's about time people kept their heads (on)!

STOP TERROR!

GAME OVER
(ITALY / NOVEMBER 2011)

He has actually gone and done it!
He's thrown the towel in,
right in the midst of an acute debt crisis.
And that to the tune of 15,000 billion Norwegian Kroner.
The end of an era, a difficult era, a nightmare era for many.
Not before time for some of us…
He had a fair crack of the whip though!
Alas, not his choice that his comrades
no longer wanted to play ball.
Echoes of Julius Caesar from here to Pompey.
He's not ready to take his bat home yet, though.
Naive are they to think that this could be his last innings!
Up and down, in and out it goes.
Now it's all out for three (terms in office).
But he's like a bad penny…
From sweepers to mega block(s) (of companies).
And he's the man on it.
What's 'under his umbrella' was evidence
that he was fit to run the country.
With sweeping reforms (?), sweeping the board,
sweeping under the carpet and both
clean and foul sweeps he's dominated politics for 17 years.
And he will have taken a fair few to the cleaners!
One of the country's richest men is no saint, he knows.
La dolce vita and 2,500 court appearances in 106 trials
in the space of 20 years and at a cost of 200 million euros.
He's proud and he's embittered,
the 'shamelessly trashy' (according to his second
wife) longest-serving post-war PM.
He's in with The Mob, some say.
Aren't they all?!
Better than being mobbed?!
The new caretaker better watch his back.
Too many cooks spoil the broth.
And, if **he** still has his spoon in it
(as a 'forza maggiore' behind the scenes)
there'll be little (positive) change.
A right old brew!

ROOM 250
(THE ABB RAMPAGE – NORWAY 2011 / 2012)

The look on that man's face is enough
to take anybody's breath away.
Exactly that!
He took their breath away.
But he didn't do himself in.
And he didn't get shot in the process of capture.
He's still around to tell the tale.
And he's loving it!
An evil contriver.

This is not 24/7, it's 22/7.
It's the imprint on the calendar of his
bomb and island killing spree.
You can think what you like, speak of it
and even write about it.
It's what you call freedom of a 'permitted' kind.
But what you can't do is stage a total shoot-out because of it!
Long gone are the days of the Wild West.
Or are they?
So many young ones on the run (from those bullets).
And now his family is (from the press).
They'll not thank him for it!
It was an act of political violence.
He was fighting for a cause, it was said.
Fighting against the 'clever manipulators',
those 'protecting and nourishing perversion'
One-track!
It was his one-shot, and he was one-up at this one-night stand.
Hopefully a one-off!
But the one-man-show has now been shown,
that his bombing and shooting frenzy has
actually had the reverse effect.
Quite a slap in the face!
Is somebody going to wipe that haunting smirk off his face, or not?
Well, if the 21-year prison sentence doesn't,
then nothing will, one might think.
But the 'reverse effect' and the complete
waste of time (and lives) will in time.
He'll certainly have a lot of that on his hands, as well as the blood…!

WSC 2012

Go big or go home!
It's sunny, blue, spectacular and beautiful.
It's super hard.
It's raw.
They're 'up and coming'.
They're hungry.
They're having fun.
They're flying like eagles.
They're falling.
They're tackling the elements. All six!
It's the best of three for the best nine.
It's BBQ – Bigger, Better, Quality.
'Put the first one down' and
'be pretty happy with it', is the message.
Keep your landings clean!
There's a mixture of all ages and heights.
Sort the men from the boys?
But the men are (still) the boys!
The music is Sweet.
It's a Blitz in this Ballroom.
And the man on skis with the camera is enjoying his job.
We're in the Oslo World Winter Capital.
It's just a bus ride away —
the World Snowboarding Championships.
And it's the last man out in the last round
who took them all to the cleaners!

SHORT-SLEEVED, BROWN AND BAGGY!

Is this my…

Pride and joy?
Love?
One and only chance?
Life?
Body?
Destiny?
Pearl of wisdom?
Moment of truth?
Crying time?
Seat?
Purpose (in life)?
Cup of tea?
Morning glory?
Life's work?
Trademark?
Curtain call?
Type?
First, last, everything?
Final straw?

Is this heading my way?

Yes, but it's just a (his) T-shirt!

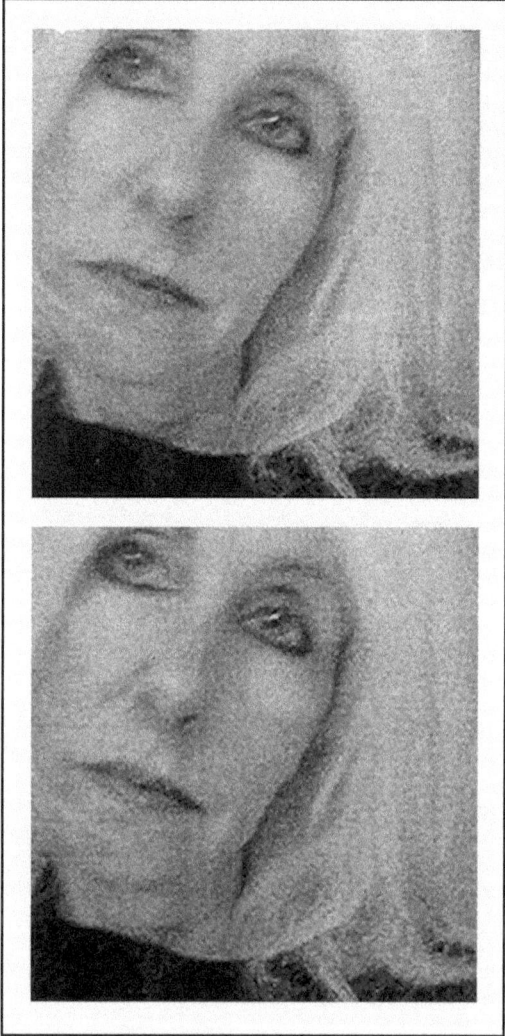

CARRYING THE TORCH FOR THE BOTH OF US!

MARIA

We haven't changed much, you and I.
Still the 'slip of a girl' times two,
like when we were tripping the light fantastic!
But a lot of water has run under the bridge,
for the both of us.
Alas, you didn't quite make it to London.
The curtains of the Olympic Theatre will go up without you.
No chance to see the best perform.
But you've been the star in your own programme.
Running your own race.
The race of your life.
Seven years of whatever it took.
Hurdle after hurdle, round after round.
Stamina and determination of a gigantic kind.
You made it into mid-life,
but we're now the ones with the crisis.
'We were good,' you said.
'We missed our way,' I said (Gaga and Jones).
The hospital bed, a far cry from the American Diner
and the best cheesecake in Manchester!
And now you're off the beaten track.
You're on another course.
You (we) filled Church House
with jazz and tap movements back in the day.
Now your body has had its fill.
And then there's your high-heeled shoes to fill?!
You've left your mark on many young learning faces.
This 'test' has left its mark on you.
No more swelling, no more exhaustion,
no more sleepless nights, for you my dear friend.
Take my scarf, my pearls, your highest heels
and look your best on your 'special' day.
We didn't cry.
Were too proud to cry.
Was too numb to cry, because you are too young to die!!!

IN LOVING MEMORY

INSPIRED BY NATURE – LONDON 2012

Inspired by 'human' nature, to be precise.
Inspired by fair-play and discipline.
It's made of sport.
It's designed for humans,
but the performance is far beyond that.
It's driven by a shared passion that goes
further than borders or limits.
It's the fruits of their efforts.
This is where the difference between 'hero' and 'zero'
is measured in microseconds.
And they can be heroes just for one day,
for much longer, or for much less.
A brave new beginning for some.
There was no willful blocking.
It was to be everyone's Olympic Games,
and where sweat, not swagger, would rule the day.
Some say they're bonkers (to push SO far),
but they're just free.
Sitting on the edge of our seats, standing to attention
and jumping for joy – we are in awe.
And now the finish line is in sight.
It was packed.
It was heaving.
A true show of public unity.
And thus they were psychologically wired (by the
electrifying crowd) to give their absolute best.
A symphony of clapping, cheering, screaming and singing.
It was everything to come, now, not what has been.
It was the best of live (coverage) and all that's alive on this planet.
It was literally 'something else'!
We were told to be prepared to get our
minds blown, and we did have.
Rule Britannia and it was so cool!

MAA – MASSIVE ATHLETE ATTACK – LONDON 2012

To the tune of We Will Rock You,
we will most certainly sock it to you.
Even though the country's really quite skint,
for the games of 2012 into our pockets we will delve,
to make this a party one will never want to shelve!
If it's points out of ten I think we should score high,
and it's congrats all round to those who
had their finger in the pie!

TO A TEE
(2012)

Right now the score is 50 off par for a telegram!
But whether it's 'at par', 'below par', 'above par'
or 'on a par with…', one thing's sure – you're my brother!
And you're a lion (in the kingdom).
The stars say that:
* You could sell sand to the Sahara if you so wished
  (with your enthusiasm and passion
  for things you're excited about).
* You show initiative.
* You've got sparkle.
* You've got intelligence and a special kind of insight.

You've also had handicaps, but you're not average.
You've certainly got drive.
And your love of motorbikes is still true.
As I remember it, you liked your music loud,
and the rock was hard,
to the tune of Rush, Deep Purple, Black Sabbath,
Led Zeppelin, AC/DC, Guns N' Roses and the likes.
We made it to a fair few concerts, you and I,
but we almost didn't make it home from the Knebworth one.
Black and yellow, or white and red,
was how you liked 'your room'.
Your monster sketches were second to none.
You were ace at ice hockey.
You've followed the Bulls.
And you've sunk a few.
First it was milk, and then it was the fluid made
from malt, sugar, hops and water.
Being headstrong, you've had your fair share
of tackles (and not just on the pitch).
Back in the day it seemed like it was 'born to be wild'.
Then it was 'born to play'.
And now it's 'born to golf'.
You followed in dad's (printing and book binding) footsteps.
You filled his shoes and became a (smooth)
skilled operator of a computerised kind.
And your shoes?
Just take them off, put your feet up and have a good one, Nigel.

FOR GOOD MEASURE

Elton John's not the only one still standing.
You are.
Yeah, yeah, yeah.
Best before date?
Is there a limit?
Anyway, you're neither the norm, nor standard.
But you're definitely in proportion.
And I recollect no need for 'made to measure'.
You've commanded that system of units (W&M).
You've inspected in an official way for
compliance with regulations.
You've examined closely for faults and errors.
You've measured the weight of all sorts.
You've added weight to all sorts, apart
from yourself (in terms of ounces).
You've dealt with the measureless and the measurable.
And what you've said/written has carried weight.
You've pulled your weight, and you've
probably thrown it around a bit!
As far as I'm concerned, you've tipped the scales!
And, on a day like today we are certainly not
going to talk about the 'weight of cares'.
A splendid 90th birthday to you, Donald.

THE TUBE: 150 YEARS IN LONDON

(2012)

It's the railway that runs in the tunnels
beneath our streets and houses.
First it was steam.
Then electric traction.
With automatic gates.
150 years in the (hood) city.
The city first built on two low, gravel-topped hills on the north bank.
The city called Londinium by the Romans.
The city where the Queen is offered the City Sword at Temple Bar.
The city that never (sleeps) stops being on
(its) guard for terrorist bombings.
An institution.
Up there with the best of them.
The buses, the telephone boxes, the taxis (cabs).
The quickest way (means) from A to Z.
The Metropolitan (now Circle)
between Paddington and Farringdon was the earliest.
There were 'inner', 'middle' and 'outer' circle services.
First there was 'cut and cover',
then there was tunnelling with the 'Greathead shield'.
Ashfield and Pick.
The 'Twopenny Tube'.
It's lengthened far into the suburbs.
It's up top as well as down below.
There's pink, blue and all the (other) colours under the (sun) ground!
Room for an average number of 60,000
people (during air raids) in WW2.
And it was 'Yardley goes with girls' at Seven Sisters
(on the Victoria line) at shortly before
half past two (2) back in the day…
Picture this.
Stifling hot, up and down, round and round.
A big black bag and a ton of books almost broke this one's bones!
Picture that.
Pretty cold, up the stairs and over.
A clumsy fall almost got this one's case
(plus worldly goods) pinched!

We're told we're not indispensable,
but, (this) THE TUBE is!

THE AGE OF ELIZABETH (LONDON 2012)

It hasn't just been plain sailing
for the lady so powerful in her permanence,
but still prepared to move with the times.
A woman, wife, mother and monarch.
The Head of Commonwealth, no less.

She has been agreed with, questioned, criticised.
She has been smiled at, waved at, cheered.
She has been admired, wondered, saluted.
She has been welcomed, accompanied, delighted.
She has received standing ovations.

But does anybody envy her?
The hard work?
The commitment?
The act of total dedication?
A life-long service from the age of 26.
A move from Heir Presumptive to accession without passing go!
A journey with the promise of a vision which brings joy,
the quality of joy in the happiness of others.

This dedicated follower of fashion has been in the glitter,
scrap, story and pop-up picture books.
A figure of glamour and purity.
Some of us have seen her from afar.
Some of us have been practically next to her.
Some of us have shaken her hand.
Some of us have given her flowers.

She rules Britannia.
Britannia rules the waves.
She rules the waves.
Six decades of living proof that public service is possible.
Her sense of humour is wonderful.
Her good old-fashioned common sense is hard to beat.
With 400 engagements per year she should
be called Elizabeth The Great!

But who would have thought it?
The elegant lady on horseback to have
to face a period of alienation!
'Annus horribilis', with the function, finance and frailties
of our reigning Queen and the other royals at issue.
Talk of 'QVS'!
As with Victoria before her,
there was only one way – UP!

This year diamonds have been the Queen's best friend.
A scintillating rise to the occasion.
And they are for ever.
She will live for ever,
on the cover of a magazine, on the stamps, on the box,
on the porcelain, on the tins, in the frames,
in the glass cases, in our minds.
And each one of us will take her with us.
The personification of the best of Britain, the best of British.
Passion, Pride, Glory.
This must be the ultimate in 'a hard act
to follow', on a global scale!

ENRAPTURED MOONSTRUCK ZOMBIE

Oh, for the (wings of a dove) leaves of a book,
said the young man when he turned up at the Antique Show
and was told that his collection of 'screens'
was practically worthless.
No increase in value, just drop in price.
Long gone were the comics, encyclopaedias,
complete works and cars, to name but four,
when he totally embraced the portable 'screen' age.
When he let it take over his life.
Nothing to keep for posterity.
Nothing to look back on and smile, laugh, cry.
Now all he wants is total recall.
You'll never know what you've got till it's gone, sings Britney.
That absolutely enraptured moonstruck
soul already knows (forever)!
Many more like him?

IO TEMO

When they take the clocks
(As we have grown up with them and learnt to love them,
Like the ones the mice ran up,
The ones great uncle Willy used to love to mend,
The ones we/they clocked in and out of,
The ones to be or not to be wound up,
The ones with or without Roman numerals,
The ones reminding us when it's summer and winter,
The ones ringing in the new,
The collectable ones,
The carriage ones,
The ones given for service rendered,
The ones telling us to rise and embrace the new day,
The ones housing a certain kind of bird and
The big one called Ben,)
Away
We will lose
All sense,
All feeling,
Of being,
Of past, present and future with
All anticipation,
All hope,
Of dreaming,
Of experimenting,
All anti-age for the modern age,
All sense of victory,
Of great anthems,
Of the sunshine of our love.
The cause will be lost.
No more plastic dreams.

IN LOVING MEMORY (WILLIAM SILVERWOOD)

RURAL PASTIME

Old MacDonald had a farm.
And on that farm he had some phones.
With a selfie here and a selfie there,
here a selfie, there a selfie,
everywhere a selfie…
until the cows come home!

Not just urban (development)!

MODERN TWIST

You gotta (pick a pocket or two) take a selfie or two, or three,
or four, or five, or six, or seven or more, Oliver.
Or you're OUT!
Friendly advice?

RED AND BLUE (I)

Roses are red,
Violets are blue.
She put out 50 selfies today.
And so did you!

More fool them!
Try being more anti**social** tomorrow!
Kick (ass) **media**!
Best, before you totally lose track of what's
going on in your own back garden…

RED AND BLUE (II)

Roses are red.
Violets are blue.
Who is the fairest of them all?
Without 50.000 'likes' it's certainly not you!

FUTURE MARKET DOMINANCE

He'll be blind by the time he's 20!
And plenty more species where that came from.
They'll be up to their eyes in (it) work!
That's what it's about – eyes!
Those ophthalmic and dispensing people
better have plenty of jam jar bottoms to choose from.
But who is going to eat all the jam?

THE MAN-IN-THE-(MIRROR)-BROWSER

Some might see themselves as lacking
in physical or mental strength.
Some might be liable to break.
Some might see themselves as lacking in firmness of character.
Some might be weak in voice.
Some might see themselves as lacking in conviction.
Some might lack flavour.
One sure thing is that many are weak in passwords,
and the man-in-the-browser is hungering for them:
your/their credentials (online)!

THEY ARE AMONG US

The fruits of our efforts and insights
will make us redundant.
They'll take the jobs,
sooner and/or later.
They are already among us…
Made to perfection by perfectionists,
only to make a mistake before my very eyes.
Still, the less we need to do,
the less we'll get to do, and
the less we'll be capable of doing…
Not so able!
History repeating?
With those looming, almost intimidating,
gigantic dinosaur-like movements
it's history reminding!

THE SOUND OF (MUSIC) SILENCE

When the Banging,
Ringing,
Clattering,
Barking,
Screaming,
Clunking,
Scraping
Howling,
Rustling,
Snorting,
Crying,
Whirring,
Squeaking,
Dripping,
Grinding,
Scratching,
Bubbling,
Spitting,
Fermenting,
Sizzling,
Whimpering,
Cracking,
Spluttering,
Babbling of the Earth's machinery stops, there will be silence.
Eventually.
'Rien ne va plus' for 'in one ear and out the other'.
Music to the ears, at last.
Golden!
For whom?
The extraterrestrial babes?!

DO STAND, BUT NOT STILL!

Take a breath.
Take a sip.
Take a bite.
Take a (peek) look.
Take a picture.
Take a step.
Take a risk.
In constant movement are we born unto this earth.
But now stop!
Take a stand
'cos if you don't you are
your own worst enemy!
No-one but yourself can save you
from the disappointment, dread,
depression, desperation
you feel in your bones of not having
said,
done,
what you actually wanted to,
what you really meant to,
what you definitely had in mind to,
what you sadly forgot to,
what you were obviously just too scared to…
And now live with it!
You don't, won't have any other choice…
until the next time?!

MORE FEMALES TAKE TO DIY IN 2014

It's on the table again.
To be, or not to be (a mother).
Now, later, not at all, not again or not any more?????
Just take it!
The right?
The embryo?
The (regret) pill?
Sisters are doing it (for) themselves and
designing unlikely futures?
They're keeping an eye on the (their) future?
One direction?
Which is it (to be)?

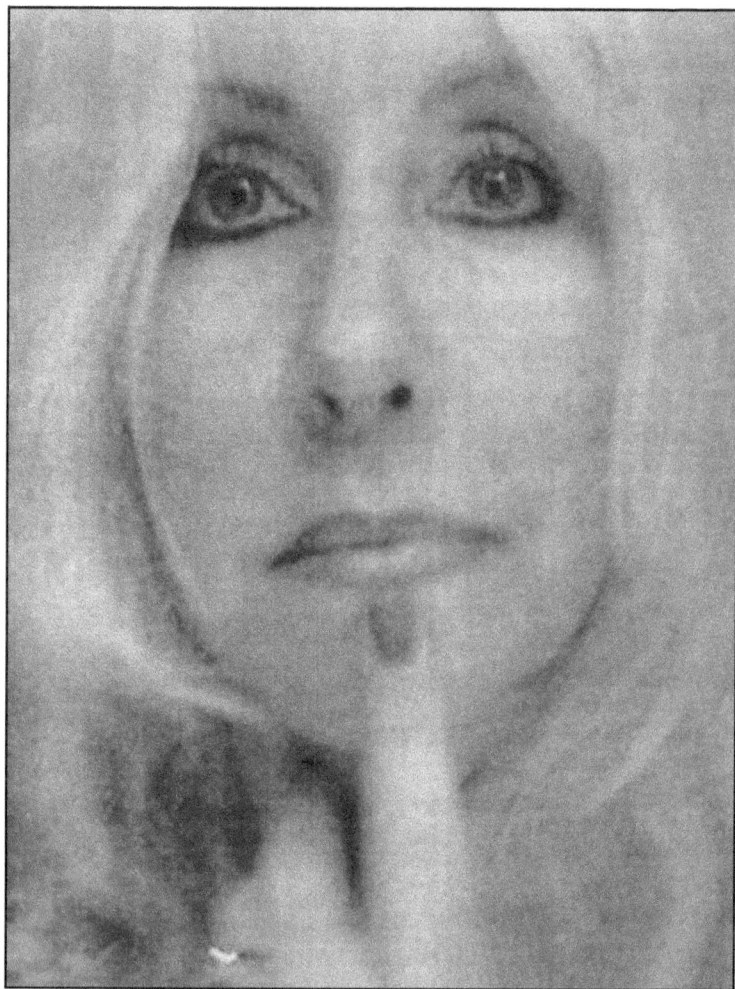

WORTH A THOUGHT, WOULDN'T YOU SAY?!

SUPERNOVA

Enjoy the shine of the sun whilst it lasts,
Who knows if you'll actually finish that bowl of soup?!

TAKE YOU TO MY DISNEYLAND ANY DAY!

I **have loved** you since forever and a day.
I **will love** you for forever and a day.
Save this planet,
it's the only one with us on it.
WWWF – wonderfully Waggish
                              Watertight
                              Worldly Family.
Answer, if you hear me!

MARGARET HILDA THATCHER
(ALIAS THE IRON LADY) FROM GRANTHAM

(2013)

Married (to Denis).
Mother of twins (Carol and Mark).
Methodist (with the courage to be).
Patron of the RCH.
Introducer of 'Thatcherism'.
Britain's longest-serving Prime Minister and a first.
The most dominant in politics of the 20th century.
Global figure.
Had a trusted companion in Denis and
was a cruel blow when she lost him.
A 'path to power"' with immense hurdles.
A lady who argued over fish 'n' chips,
personified economic 'good housekeeping'
and 'living within (your) her means',
reached out to the young and those who were 'not important'.
The print unions and the miners (up North), who said their piece.
A bitter rise in unemployment followed by
a sweet re-take of the Falklands (and wealth).
She put the country back on track.
Into the fresh.
"Look at us now," she said.
She showed courage, steadfastness and did right for the common good.
"You can turn if you like, but this lady's not for turning," she said.
A lot of DDC – dignity, diligence, courtesy.
She saved the (MI6) spy who loved (me) them,
but she couldn't save his marriage
(after a massive attack on the Kremlin).
His life had no meaning,
but she said "there is always hope."
2,300 representing 170 countries.
The flag and white flowers.
A military air with full honours.
When the wall fell she had been there to honour it,
when she was 'subject to common destiny'
the Queen (herself) was in St Paul's to honour her.

Baroness Thatcher – both loved and hated,
but 'there when our country needed it most'.
An iconic political figure and
'the loving mother always in (our) their hearts'.

IN MEMORY

I AM WHAT I AM
(SINCE 1998)

One life (on this earth).
One heck of a love of life, Joshua.
Born elsewhere, but well-rooted in God's own country.
The selfsame grit and love for the rhythm.
And you've already had to face the music!
There will be many crossroads and signposts.
Take the right direction.
What's right for you,
the one who strongly greets.
But never run faster than your guardian angel(s) can fly!
And when you are boarding through the ruts
of this over-competitive, over-consumptive,
'speak before you think', but truly magnificent, world of ours,
keep on the straight, but don't be narrow (minded)!
Not regular and complex, but goofy and
quite the opposite you are.
Use your head but have a heart.
And home will always be where your heart is.
Full of joy, peace, harmony and your 'epic' storms.
Dare to rule/be the centre, but not self-centred.
Love others, but also love yourself.
Leave Off Very Evil!
You have been told the ancient things.
Use your knowledge and (many) talents wisely.
Not everyone has such a fire inside.
Let yours burn, but not out.
Fortune favours the brave, they say.
So you will most certainly be loaded…
And, you shall never, never, never be a slave!

THE LIFE OF BRIAN

It's not Monty Python,
it's Brian F.
Professionally you were in oil.
I believe it was industrial.
Otherwise, you're very fondly remembered
by your bridge and golfing friends.
And there was many a happy time
spent with Jean and Derrick,
with M&S desserts in great abundance.
A very generous sort of a man.
A very decent sort of a man.
A very medium-sized sporty sort of a man,
with a very gigantic-sized smile.
It didn't light up the cold war, but everything else.
And one never knew if you
were joking until you did, SMILE.
We took our lives in our hands
when we were out with you on the open roads.
It was nought to 100 before we knew where we were!
In the end it was driving and your health that made you
and the whole family move nearer to the sea.
Heaven was still Yorkshire, though!
But there were to be no more
starters à la Operatic Safari Supper at yours after that.
So that was the life of you, Brian.
You came and you went.
But your (closest) followers are still in the world.
Courtesy dies hard; it just lives on.
May you (continue to) beam (down) on them each and every day.

IN LOVING MEMORY

I'M (A) MOBILE (SINCE 1973)
(2013)

Just about everyone is surfing these days.
But it's not on a long board.
It's not on water.
It's not only in warm places.
There are waves though, and plenty of them.
I started out weighing in at around a bag of sugar.
A battery life of 20 minutes.
It was with this that Martin Cooper gave Joel Engel
a bell from Sixth Avenue, NYC.
It was April, but he was no fool.
And just look at me now!
Touch screens, megapixel cameras,
Android OS v 4 (ice cream sandwich),
MG, GB, smart telephones, android OS 2.3
(Gingerbread), SIM, IOS 6, A6 – chips and more.
Phone, messages, calendar, photos, videos,
music, games, maps, weather, news, notes,
reminders, clock, alarm, mail, App Store,
and the list goes on.
As slim as it gets?
Maybe not.
There's still room to further slenderise.
In use since 1973.
And I'm still going places.
I'm connecting people anywhere and everywhere.
Mountain high, valley low,
uniting loved ones, closing deals.
Happy birthday, to (you) me!

MARTIN
(A MAN FOR ALL COURSES)

You lost your dad young.
Long before his time.
You lost your sister.
Long before her time.
Your mum lost you (too).
Long before your time.

All long before their time!

Almost three (3) years of
wining and dining the angels
to your credit, already!
'Gentle, warm, smiley, fun, lovely, cuddly'
on earth as (it is) you will be in heaven.
'Missed' on earth.

May peace be in your soul.

IN LOVING MEMORY

SOCHI 2014
(THE PUTIN GAMES)

Impeccable.
Definitely the athletes' games, by all accounts.
Most probably not the people's games,
seeing as how most couldn't afford to get anywhere near them.
And there was a lot to wonder and amaze over.
98 events, as opposed to 61 in 1994.
I like blue, but not at any price.
Inflated to 330 billion Norwegian Kroner.
Money, money, money…
in a poor man's world.
Quite seriously, just how much un-drunk Powerade
was chucked in the space of 17 days?
Where do we go from here?
Is the 'foundation' in all its crucial importance now shaking?

ARGENT
(INSPIRED BY THE SCULPTURE 'GRIPPING' BY RICHARD DEACON)

(NORWAY 2014)

Conspicuous in its magnificence.
Company to the cave,
the eyes behind a thousand windows,
smoke feeling its way up to the vault of heaven.
A cascade of raw and glance.
Swan-like.
Urban elegance.
Tenure.
Taking mental possession of today and tomorrow.
Shining with a tremulous light of fear,
anxiety, excitement and hope.
The urban clutch.
Joining together our bodies, holding together our souls
as we climb, merely sit a while or just sit it out…
Possession of understanding and mastery.
Mass domination of the elbowroom we all need
between (the devil) HiG and the (deep blue sea) Mjøsa.
Gripping.

YOU SAY WHAT?!

On the road at seven.
In the dark, so soon upon us.
I turned, to be startled by a shadow.
Mine.
No story about true love and weather.
That Russian roulette moment of truth.
That aftertaste of power-play antics.
Hard to grasp.
Harder to accept.
Hardest to put in front of me.

SHOULD OLD ACQUAINTANCE BE FORGOT?
(ON THIS THE EVE OF DESTRUCTION)

SCOTLAND 2014

Is it really about who Andy Murray will play for?
No longer will there be having a drink and getting together,
just sourness.
A sharp biting taste of mega-magnitude to the lips.
A sentence?
Picture (this) that!
Anyone for tennis?
For auld lang syne!

FATEFUL AVALANCHE
(SCOTLAND 2014)

NO means YES.
YES means NO.
From us and them to you and me (and them).
United we stand, divided we (all) fall
(at or on some point).
I **prefer** your fabulous clothes to your
opinion on the 'decision', Viv.
Just watch that snow(ball-effect)!
Where might it **end**?
Could well turn out to be a dumd**um**!

Viv = Vivienne Westwood

THE DAY THE TREE LEFT US
(NORWAY 2014)

Quite suddenly.
They drove in (to town).
Out of nowhere.
Two men in suits.
Looking like ebola!
It was a long, painful (to the ear) process.
Like a lamb to the slaughter – dismembered and milled
before my very window(s).
Dismay.
Silence after.
And the season of goodwill?!
Monday morning blues made worse…!

ONE FOR THE ROAD

Maybe high-flying birds
Are chasing yesterday,
But pavement crawlers
Are trying not to choke
On visions of tomorrow's shadows.

GENERAL ELECTION 2015

Roses are red,
Violets are blue,
What will it be,
New or you?
It's you, for another five of term (office).

You want to bring our country together.
It's thumbs up for the sweetest victory yet.
Your job's secured and you feel so passionate about it.
The possibility to serve our country again needs to be celebrated.
It was 326 for an overall (outright) majority and you got it!

Milliband is taking the can (for the loss).
It wasn't his night.
He thanks those for pounding the streets.
He thanks the British people for meeting him on train stations.
He may be gone by lunchtime, but Labour will continue
to fight for the working class.
The issue of our unequal country will not go away.
A cruel night for the Liberal Democrats.
So heartbreaking to see the results.
And UKIP's leader never felt happier.
With a clean sweep for the SNP (in Scotland)
the Scottish lion has roared.

And yet again, David William Donald Cameron's quite shell-shocked.
So are the staff at No 10.
He's en route to see the Queen once more.
He knows the way.
Keep this kingdom united.
Keep Britain great.
We owe it to those before you.
Govern (all) with respect.
We owe it to those after you.
We need a strong man with a party.
You are strong.
A man of distinction and conviction,
on the brink of something special.
And just remember —
there's plenty of talent (unrivalled skills and creativity),
working people with such good humour, compassion
and mouths to feed NOT ONLY SOUTH of Watford Gap!

HAPPY MEN (FRANCE WWI)

Happy men are these who secured
the safety of the nation (for the likes of us).
The men Wilfred was to write about.
James and the other lads.
The Cameron Highlanders.
He was an event that happened.
They were an event that happened.
He chose what to follow.
They chose what to follow.
It was 'Your Country Needs You'!
And with all the uncertainty of what lay ahead.
Blind loyalty?
Greater love hath no man than this.
What was his reward?
Between the devil and the deep blue sea.
To slide and slither.
To cough like a hag.
To hurtle downwards towards oblivion.
In motion endlessly.
Where darkness was not just an absence of light.
Where appalling carnage blotted out the stars
and memories sweet of summer under
those trees beside the park.
Where hopes and dreams were trodden into dust by the enemy.
The ceaseless hatred of the sky.
What we are dealing with here is a total
lack of respect for (the law) life!
For the next generation of men.
For the next generation of lovers.
For the next generation of fathers (to next
generation wee girls and boys).
For the next generation of breadwinners.
Our men with recurrent rash irritations.
Our men marching asleep.
Guttering, choking, drowning.

Our men with screams of 'maniac earth',
blood-curdling enough to silence all that's ever been said.
As if the world was on fire to them!
Not just of the enemy did this war take its so very heavy toll!
Little comfort that I marched through those same trenches.
Alas, no rifle over my shoulder.
No slipping and grasping in vain.
No wipers.
No bloodbath.
But, with an interested eye and peace ruling the day.
Surrounded by allies.
Those who hurt others hurt themselves more,
but these poor souls had but one choice.
Invaders must (die) be stopped!
Invaders of the peace.
Invaders of peace of (his) mind.
Ninety years of mourning and marking
with poppies this very day
for him and others who kissed the stones.
His body is surely there to be found, somewhere.
In a French field.
He didn't have much time to pack up his troubles
in his old kitbag and smile, smile, smile.
Heaven's gates opened so early to his soul.
Too young to not have all the time in (the) this world!

IN LOVING MEMORY (JAMES SCADE)

DARLINGS (OF THE NATION)
(WW2)

(INSPIRED BY MORMORMONOLOGENE /
THE GRANDMOTHER MONOLOGUES
BY KAROLINE HJORTH – VIDEO)

They didn't secure it,
they kept it going.
When the cats were away,
the mice didn't have time to play much.
They rolled their sleeves up and got down to some hard graft.
The backbone.
Whilst the men were playing sailor, soldier, spy,
whilst the men were digging and flying for victory,
the women were playing tinker, tailor, nurse
and just about everything else.
They were making ends meet,
when they hardly could/did!
Little or no food, but no starved imagination.
The Homefront.
They pulled together.
Sisters helped sisters, whatever their station.
Female carriers and packers.
So, what are these pearls of wisdom doing now?
These grandmothers?
Keeping fit.
Doing crossword puzzles.
Having their hair permed.
Dusting their photo frames.
Brewing their tea and keeping abreast with the TV.

Eating bread and cheese and jam.
Meeting for coffee and putting the world to rights.
Tending to their plants.
Sorting their tablets (into a box).
Feeling comfortable in their socks, slippers
and flowery dressing-gowns.
Still giving good advice!
Some don't smile as much as they used to.
Some just don't like what we have done with their/our cosmos!
Some have regrets. Some don't.
Some are social. Some are not.
Some are forever estranged. Some are forever connected.
Some have a restless yearning tugging at their souls.
Three cheers, that they made the (war) effort!
They were/are worth their weight in gold.
But which government can afford to (re)pay that?!
Alas, don't write them off like some bad loan,
when those left need it most!

ACHTUNG BABY

I hate to remind you,
but if those Tommies and Jocks
hadn't given you a helping hand,
you'd have been speaking Deutsch
and eating Bockwurst
for as long as you can remember!

THE ONES WHO GOT AWAY
(WW1 / WW2)

They came back.
But did they ever?
They got away from it all.
Sooner or later.
With or without wounds to nurse.
With burnt offerings of senses.
But what did they get back to?
Another planet for them.
Not able to forget.
Not able to adjust.
Not able to accept.
These were pleasant men.
These were peaceful men.
These were men who had loved laughter.
These were talented men.
These were men with futures before them, behind them.
These were caring men with a need for care, attention, direction.
Some wallowed in it, the pity of war.
Some lost it.
Some took it, and so committed a crime (back then).
No repair for the war's damage.
The mystery of courage destroyed.
The mastery of wisdom silenced.
Sleeplessness and mayhem.
No procedure to move back into the sun.
Some of us never got the chance to meet the
grandfathers we should have had.
Alas, cruel compensation manifests itself in
the form of that picture on the wall.

IN LOVING MEMORY (CLARENCE SILVERWOOD)

VICTOIRE
(70TH ANNIVERSARY OF LIBERATION DAY / 2015)

And at the proclaimed end,
Freedom, freedom, freedom, they cried.
Vive la différence.
That's what they did – made that difference.
They freed them.
They freed us all.
May we be truly thankful, grateful, humble
Before them, before their memory
Until the end of (our) time.

WEAR YOUR POPPY WITH PRIDE
(REMEMBRANCE 2015)

One hundred years of conflict.
A sombre day,
but not cold.
Flowers Of The Forest,
Nimrod and
Oh What A Lovely War!
So many young men
stepped forward to serve.
For the protection of our way of life.
So many young men still
step forward to serve.
For us to be free.
For this day and always.
Listen to the silence.
See the damage.
The glorious dead.
Our glorious dead.

TIME FOR A BIT MORE?

LIVE AND LET LIVE (LALL) DATING AGENCY 2010
CHECK THIS SITE OUT!

Online Dating / Speed Dating / Blind Date Dating /
Walk In The Park Dating / High Tea Dating /
Training Partner Dating

Looking for the (this) one?

Perfect Partner (I)
Likes red.
Has control.
Is confident.
Does karate.
Eats (junk) food when possible.
Doesn't get much sleep.

Perfect Partner (II)
Likes purple.
Is untidy.
Is not confident, but efficient.
Doesn't do any sport whatsoever.
Eats pizza.
Can't sleep much.

Perfect Partner (III)
Likes pink and glitter.
Has stuff all over the place.
Is shy.
Is used to being told what to do.
Eats salad and very little else.
Has no time to sleep.

Perfect Partner (IV)
Likes blue.
Has everything folded and in its place.
Is conservative.
Is bossy.
Eats French (cordon bleu) food.
Goes to bed at the same time every night.

Perfect Partner (V)
Likes (bright) white.
Has nothing under control.
Is careful/sceptical.
Likes to cycle (mountain bike).
Eats fish.
Stays up late.

Perfect Partner (VI)
Likes black.
Has everything under control.
Is open and friendly.
Likes to work out at the gym.
Eats taco.
Has a normal sleeping routine.

INTERESTED?

SINGLED OUT

To be able to prove his identity he had to help them identify the identity of another man, who had been travelling on the same bus as him since leaving the identification parade, who actually had no identity to identify, according to the identification system the Old Bill was using to identify the identities of such unidentifiable persons, dead or alive, past or present.

THE DOG BIT THE (DUST) BOY

They hadn't been there more than five minutes before it happened again! Mum and dad didn't even have time to check in before there was a scream outside. A panic-stricken mum managed to blurt out that he should never have touched the dog. Dad was equally as irritated.

The son was bleeding. There was a lot of blood. It had bitten him at the side. Of his mouth. Quite a challenge for any hound!

Off to the hospital they went. As luck would have it, the daughter found herself with strangers whilst her brother was being doctored! They were very nice, though.

LOST IN FRANCE

It was the trip they had all been looking forward to. They were to explore northern France. The headmaster was on board (with it) and actually on the bus (with them)!

What with nighties as dresses, the worst food you could imagine and a ban on too many sweets (to fill up on) it wasn't quite what she'd expected. Not much fun, in fact. It was spending more time in school, another school, you see.

And it was going to get a whole lot worse. After being bullied into a prank she found her entire collection of underwear on the ground three storeys below. Talk about dirty washing! Tipped straight out of the window, they were.

I don't know about 'lost in France', it was more like a strong case of 'aghast in France', one could say.

MIDNIGHT EXPRESS

It was well past her bedtime. It was well past anyone's bedtime by the time she arrived at that little spot on the map, and after a very long and humid journey!

She'd touched down after a fairly pleasant flight. She'd secured a taxi, and the price. She'd eaten pizza in the restaurant in the very middle of the railway station. She'd made her way to the platform. But the case was irritatingly heavy and it was still so warm. And if the train would actually pull in, and where, was anybody's guess.

There'd obviously been a change of plan. Heads were turning and tongues were being set in motion at a very fast pace, or so it seemed to her. She was still getting to grips with the lingo.

Eventually, she did find herself hanging out of the carriage window, as it was rattling its way along the coastline. And it was indeed breathtaking!

JUST JILL WENT UP THE HILL (I)

Sister Jill went up the hill
instead of going to Ibiza.
Jill fell down and consequently met a preacher,
who tried to reach her to cushion her fall,
which functioned well considering he was tall.
The next thing they did was to find a ball,
seeing as how they were sporty and
not more than forty, in the sun!
They had lots of fun until the pizza was done.
Then they went home and spoke on the phone,
seeing as how they were once more alone,
each in his/her separate house,
like cat and mouse,
'cos they couldn't be together…

JUST JILL WENT UP THE HILL (II)

Sister Jill went up the hill
to meet a certain teacher.
Jill fell down and, as luck would have it, met a preacher,
who had tried to reach her
to write a feature about a creature
he'd listened to at confession,
a part of his profession.

The moral: Nothing is holy in this world of ours?!

SWEET PEA

The whole thing was quite shady. Sweet-but-sour!
You led her to that caravan. Not so large,
but enclosed. An extra trailer.
Like a lamb to the slaughter, she followed. But
it didn't come to that. She thought better of it.
You sat her down, but before you knew it
she was disappearing back out the door.
It hadn't even bothered you that all eyes were upon you (both).
I mean, you walked up to it in broad
daylight, at your own sweet will,
and they were all sitting there, chatting, knitting!

SUNDAY BLOODY SUNDAY

It was just like any other Sunday afternoon until they heard glass shattering across the street. There was a young female on the ground directly under a third-storey broken window!

It was obvious that she was going to land in Intensive Care. And he was making a quiet and very quick getaway out of a door and down the same street. The other female watching him from above was extremely disconcerted. Her partner wasn't at all sure about calling the police, but she was. She did.

To this very day she still remembers how he was large, very dark and had no shoes. The female on the ground was naked and had red ones on! No Sunday stroll, this one!

MESSAGE IN A BOTTLE

There was every currency under the sun in that bottle. Foolish indeed to agree to look after it whilst the friends were on their holidays. The two of them were actually going away at the same time! There was opportunity for a break in?!

Well hidden in the cellar, being better than hidden in the apartment, was the conclusion.

So, they travelled. Upon their return it was gone!

There would be no contact with the police. Instead, one of the friends (with the most to lose) went on and on about it on the phone. She'd make sure that they wouldn't hear the last of it, that **she'd** certainly get her money's worth!

FACTS AND FIGURES

It was a fact that she certainly had the right figure. That she'd managed to keep it was a fact well proven. But the fact of the matter is that it figures – she'd always been that way. And she was good at figures, a fact which most people just couldn't figure out. It was a fact of life that 'they' had often been distorted in her case and 'cases'. There were facts that didn't figure at all and figures that were not fact. And she'd once again have to digest, accept and live with that one – that fact, in fact!

SNOW FUN PROJECT

He'd been looking forward to it for ages. There was the usual build-up to the annual rail jam. The lights. The music. The sausages. The energy drinks. The give-aways. The adrenalin rush...

Alas, they'd raised the bar! He wasn't allowed to compete! Disappointing, unfair and tiresome were but a few of the words blurted out. And a 'sneak preview' on his own the day before was not what he had had in mind!

To be a sport, he went down for a look anyway. Then, as luck would have it, he was soon back up the road to get his gear on!

WHEN ONE DOOR CLOSES...
(2010)

Many doors are closed. For you who cannot speak the language.
Many doors are closed. For you who can speak the language!

Impossible to have a foot in the door. For
you who cannot speak the language.
Highly unlikely to get a foot in the door, let alone
keep it in. For you who can speak the language!

And, when one door closes another door opens.
For you who can speak the language.
No, wrong. When one door shuts they all shut. For
you who can or cannot speak the language!

MIND OVER MATTER

Mind your step, and whilst you are at it mind how you go, and mind your manners into the bargain, and don't forget to mind your (own) business (nobody else will), whilst at the same time minding your lip, and last but certainly not least,
mind your mother!

Six sure steps to success!

THAT BUS MUST HAVE TURNED UP AFTER ALL OR
WAS IT 'JUST BEAM HER UP THEN, SCOTTY'?

UNTIL NEXT TIME!

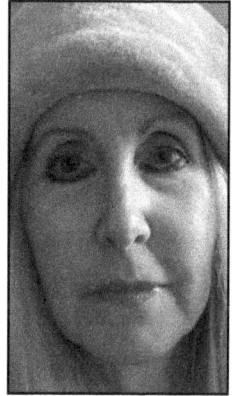

Fact File:

Name: Grit

Born: Bradford, England

Lives: Back in England

Educated in: Foreign Languages & Business Studies, Leeds
                   Polytechnic (now Leeds Metropolitan University)
                   Banking, DAG Schule (Frankfurt, Germany)
                   Teaching, HiHm (Hamar and Nesna, Norway)

Writing: Poems and all sorts

My Motto: If you feel you have something to say don't merely
                   take it to the grave!

Why Do I Write? I love it / I want to excite, provoke, shock, convince,
                   make you laugh, make you stop and think

Other Interests: Art, music, being creative (various genre), admiring
                   the countryside

www.ingramcontent.com/pod-product-compliance
Lightning Source LLC
Chambersburg PA
CBHW040804150426
42813CB00056B/2650